APTERA

Tom Warhol

Marshall Cavendish
Benchmark
New York

Other Marshall Cavendish Offices:
Marshall Cavendish International (Asia) Private Limited, 1 New Industrial Road, Singapore 536196 • Marshall Cavendish International (Thailand) Co Ltd. 253 Asoke, 12th Flr, Sukhumvit 21 Road, Klongtoey Nua, Wattana, Bangkok 10110, Thailand • Marshall Cavendish (Malaysia) Sdn Bhd, Times Subang, Lot 46, Subang Hi-Tech Industrial Park, Batu Tiga, 40000 Shah Alam, Selangor Darul Ehsan, Malaysia

Marshall Cavendish is a trademark of Times Publishing Limited

All websites were available and accurate when this book was sent to press.

Library of Congress Cataloging-in-Publication Data

Warhol, Tom.
Aptera / by Tom Warhol.
p. cm. — (Green cars)
Includes bibliographical references and index.
Summary: Provides information on the green technology used in the Aptera, and discusses how the green movement is affecting the auto industry — Provided by publisher.
ISBN 978-1-60870-008-0
1. Hybrid electric cars--Juvenile literature. 2. Aptera Motors--Juvenile literature. I. Title.
TL221.15.W36 2011
629.22'93—dc22
2009041723

Editor: Megan Comerford
Publisher: Michelle Bisson
Art Director: Anahid Hamparian
Series Designer: Daniel Roode

Illustrations on pp. 22–23 by Alanna Ranellone

Photo research by Connie Gardner

Cover photo by Mike Blake/CORBIS

The photographs in this book are used by permission and through the courtesy of: Aptera: 8, 11, 18, 20, 26, 28, 32, 34, 37, 38, 40, 41; Corbis: Mike Blake, 13, 31.

Printed in Malaysia (T)
135642

Contents

Introduction

Most cars in the world run on gasoline, and some cars use more gas than others. Gasoline is made from petroleum, or crude oil, which is a liquid buried deep in the earth. Petroleum formed naturally from the **decomposed** and **compressed** remains of tiny **organisms** that lived millions of years ago. Humans drill deep into the earth to take the oil out.

However, the amount of oil in the world is limited. The more we take out of the ground now, the less there will be in the future, and eventually it will run out. Taking it out of the ground is expensive and damages the **environment**.

Also, when oil and the products made from oil (gasoline, engine oil, heating oil, and diesel fuel) are burned, they give off pollution in the form of gases, such as carbon dioxide (CO_2). Carbon dioxide and other **greenhouse gases** damage Earth's **atmosphere**.

As the sun shines down on Earth, it first passes through the planet's atmosphere. Much of this sunlight is absorbed by the ground and water. Some of it is reflected back up into space. As more and more greenhouse gases build up in the atmosphere, they stop this reflected sunlight from leaving the atmosphere. Instead, it gets bounced back to Earth. As a result, our planet's temperature has risen, causing **global climate change.**

In the United States, about 90 percent of the greenhouse gases we produce is from burning oil, gasoline, and coal. One-third of this comes from the engines that power the vehicles we use to move people and objects around. If we do not slow or stop this global climate change, life on Earth could begin to get very uncomfortable.

A changing climate might cause some animals that can't adapt to the new conditions to die out (go extinct). Plants and crops might no longer be able to grow where people need them. As the planet's temperature increases, the sea ice and glaciers at the North and South poles may melt more, causing the sea level to rise. Many islands, low-lying countries, and communities along the coasts of all the continents might disappear into the sea.

Doesn't sound so good, does it? These problems are why many people are interested in **alternative fuels** that can power our cars and other engines with less or no pollution.

Now that you know that oil is made from living things that died a long time ago, it should be no surprise that people are making oil from live plants to power their cars. This fuel, called *biodiesel*, can be made from oils extracted from soybeans, canola, sunflowers, and other plants. Biodiesel is similar to the vegetable oil used for cooking. Some people gather or buy this used oil from restaurants and use it to power their cars. These cars' engines have to be modified, or changed, in order to burn this oil correctly.

Another popular way to power cars is with batteries. Modern batteries are so powerful that some cars use them in combination with gas engines; this system is called *hybrid technology*. Hybrid cars have both a gas engine and an electric motor. The electric motor usually takes over when the car runs at low speeds or when it stops.

Many auto engineers are designing electric cars, such as the Aptera, that run on batteries alone. Until recently, too many batteries were needed to make this an **efficient** technology. But there have been many recent advances in battery technology.

Another form of alternative energy for cars is the hydrogen **fuel cell**, which gives off power when the hydrogen and oxygen in the fuel cell are combined. However, hydrogen fuel cells are expensive to make, and there would have to be many hydrogen fueling stations along U.S. roads before people could begin driving hydrogen-powered cars.

Oil is a limited resource, costs a lot to extract, pollutes the earth and air, and forces most countries to rely on the few nations that have a plentiful supply of it. If the world wants to become a cleaner, safer place, developing alternative fuels to power at least some of our vehicles is extremely important.

Aptera Motors is working on this problem right now, and they have two car models using electric and hybrid technology very near to being on the market. The introduction of the Aptera onto American roads might change the way we think about cars!

Chapter 1
Rethinking the Car

The future is here. If you've seen the latest *Star Trek* movie, which shows the early life of James Kirk, Spock, and the other original crew members of the starship *Enterprise*, you've seen the Aptera. The electric car was featured in the movie as the vehicle driven around the campus of Starfleet Academy.

Believe it or not, these cars—the Aptera 2 series—weren't designed for a futuristic movie set, but for today's city streets. And they'll be available soon. How is this possible? Because of a lot of smart, outside-the-box thinking and a desire to use the least amount of fossil fuel possible.

◀ **On streets full of sedans and SUVs, it's hard not to notice the Aptera. It's eye-catching from every angle!**

Despite popular thinking, an all-electric car is not a new idea. In fact, electric cars were some of the earliest automobiles made. The first electric vehicle, a train, was invented in the 1830s. Then, in the 1880s, the first electric car came along. Companies started manufacturing electric cars manufactured for the general public shortly thereafter. They became so popular that more people drove electric cars than gasoline-powered vehicles in Europe and America up until the 1920s, when large amounts of oil were found in the American West and in the Middle East.

These vast new reserves of oil made gasoline-powered cars more economical than electric cars, meaning they cost less to drive. Engineers focused on building gas-powered cars, and electric cars were left in the dust.

However, now that oil is becoming harder to find and getting more expensive, several small companies and even some of the big car manufacturers are working on building an efficient electric car that is cheap to run.

Problems—including battery weight and size, run time, and the lack of charging stations—have made the large-scale manufacture of all-electric vehicles difficult to achieve. That is, until the Aptera came along.

In March 2009 Aptera Motors employees brought the Aptera 2e to Washington, D.C., to protest the car's exclusion from the Department of Energy's loan program for fuel-efficient vehicles. Members of Congress and tourists took the opportunity to ride in the 2e.

THE ULTIMATE GREEN CAR

The Aptera 2 series includes the 2e, an all-electric car, and the 2h, a series hybrid. A series hybrid is a type of vehicle in which power is provided by an electric motor that is assisted by a gasoline-powered generator. When the batteries powering the motor run low on charge, the generator starts and charges the batteries while the vehicle is still in motion.

The *2* indicates the car can carry two passengers. The *e* stands for "electric" and the *h* for "hybrid." The Aptera 2e and 2h are considered to be some of the most fuel-efficient cars ever made.

Aptera Motors, the company that developed and produces the Aptera, has achieved this energy efficiency by building the car to be as **aerodynamic** as possible. This means that the shape of the car enables air to pass easily over its body, causing less **friction**. The company called the car *Aptera*, which is Greek for "wingless flight," because the car "flies" on the ground.

One problem electric-car manufacturers have often had is that the weight of the car requires a lot of battery power. According to Aptera Motors CEO Paul Wilbur, a four-wheeled Aptera would be 34 percent less fuel efficient than the current three-wheeled design. To carry the extra weight of a four-wheeled model, the car would need a battery 50 percent larger.

Aptera Motors founders Chris Anthony (*left*) and Steve Fambro stand in front of the Aptera.

The Aptera's designers even made the wheels themselves more aerodynamic by enclosing them in their own casings. This allows the air to flow over and past them more easily instead of getting caught up in the spokes of the rims. Also, the wheels are low-rolling resistance tires, which reduce the amount of friction the tires generate against the road, resulting in higher energy efficiency.

In another nod to aerodynamics, the headlights and windshield wipers, which catch a lot of air on normal cars, are set into the surface so that they further reduce **drag**.

All of these aerodynamic and weight design ideas have allowed the Aptera 2e to achieve an amazing fuel-efficiency rating of 340 miles per gallon (145 kilometers per liter), according to the company's estimates. That's almost seven times the average fuel rating for the Toyota Prius. (Although the 2e doesn't use gasoline, miles per gallon is still used to compare it with most other cars, which do run on gas.)

The 2e can go 120 miles (193 km) on a single charge, at a cost per mile of 1.5 cents (based on a gas price of $2.67 per gallon). This is far better than every other car on the market today, from the big, bulky 6-cylinder, front-wheel-drive Chevy Equinox SUV (13.4 cents per mile) to the incredibly fuel-efficient Toyota Prius hybrid (5.36 cents per mile).

What a Drag

According to company founder Steve Fambro, an entire 1,500-pound (680-kilogram) Aptera produces less drag than just the side-view mirror of a pickup truck or Lance Armstrong on his racing bike. This means that the Aptera is extremely aerodynamic.

Engineers can measure how aerodynamic a vehicle is by measuring its drag. The measurement of this drag, or air resistance, acting on a traveling object is called the *drag coefficient*. For example, the Aptera has a drag coefficient of 0.15, which is the lowest of any car on the market. In comparison, the Toyota Prius has a drag coefficient of 0.25.

The shape of a vehicle is one of the main factors that determine how aerodynamic a car is. Boxier cars have a higher drag coefficient, while sleeker, rounded cars have a lower one. Race cars, which are always very slim and low to the ground, are more aerodynamic. This means they produce less drag and can therefore move faster.

Because the teardrop-shaped Aptera glides so smoothly through the air, when the driver's foot is off the accelerator the car doesn't jolt to a slower speed as most other cars do. Instead, the Aptera settles into a coast and gradually slows down.

The company's green philosophy goes beyond fuel efficiency and emissions. Many of the materials used in the Aptera are ecofriendly. The seat covers and flooring are made from recycled plastic bottles and colored using organic dyes. Even the steering wheel is made from recycled materials. Also, the interior lights use low-energy light-emitting diodes (LEDs).

The Aptera 2e was one of the first cars to be entered in the Progressive Insurance Automotive X Prize, which is a competition to create superefficient vehicles to reduce America's dependence on oil. The three top winners will share the $10 million prize.

AN IMAGINATIVE IDEA

While stuck in packed Los Angeles traffic, Aptera Motors cofounder Steve Fambro started thinking about all the wasted fuel and how much better it would be to zip around the city's highways and streets in a zero-emissions, highly efficient car. He couldn't stop thinking about it.

Eventually he contacted a friend of his, a boatbuilder named Chris Anthony, who loved the idea. He brought to the venture his experience with boatbuilding and his knowledge of the unique materials used for boats. That's where the idea for the Aptera's lightweight yet extremely strong chassis, or frame, came from. The Aptera's chassis is made from the same material used to make boats, which can withstand impacts and strong water pressure.

Fambro and Anthony joined forces and approached Idealab, an investment company, for financial support. Idealab's founder, Bill Gross, was psyched about the idea and invested in the new company, called Aptera Motors.

Fambro and Anthony then assembled a team of engineers and began to make their dream a reality. Work got underway in 2006. Aptera Motors grew, and was almost ready to release its first production models after about four years.

Chapter 2

Charge and Go!

The Aptera series cars are front-wheel-drive, two-passenger vehicles with plenty of trunk space. They also feature a space behind the front seats where a baby seat can be placed.

The 2e and the 2h might look the same, but don't be fooled. The two models are quite different from one another. The difference is in how each model is powered: one by electric power alone, the other by a hybrid system.

◄ **A three-wheeled design and the butterfly-style doors give the Aptera a futuristic look. Having a single rear wheel helps make the car more fuel efficient than four-wheeled cars.**

POWERING THE APTERA
Aptera 2e

The Aptera 2e is the all-electric model, which means it runs solely on batteries—rechargeable batteries, that is (specifically, ones that use lithium iron phosphate). These batteries are located below the floor of the vehicle, further reducing the Aptera's bulk and helping to keep the car stable.

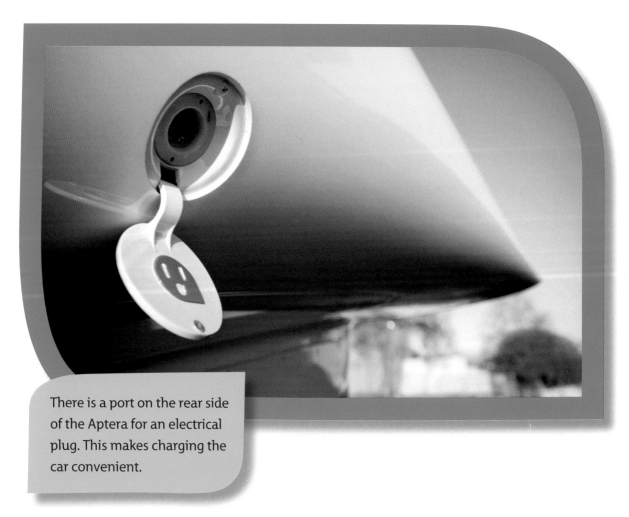

There is a port on the rear side of the Aptera for an electrical plug. This makes charging the car convenient.

The batteries can be recharged by plugging the Aptera into a regular wall outlet like those in your house. If you use a standard 110-volt outlet, the batteries can be fully recharged overnight, but if you plug it into a 220-volt outlet (like the outlets used for electric washers and dryers), it will take only four hours to give the car a full charge.

An optional quick-charger can be purchased; it reduces charging time to two to three hours. (The company doesn't give information on the life of the battery—how long it lasts before it needs to be replaced—but rechargeable batteries do need to be replaced at some point.)

To make charging even cooler, the Aptera's taillights become charge-level indicators so that the owner can easily see when the car is fully charged.

Some people think that all-electric cars can't be fast. Well, the Aptera series cars can **accelerate** from 0 to 60 miles per hour (0 to 97 kilometers per hour) in less than 10 seconds. The Aptera can reach a respectable speed of 90 miles per hour (145 km/h).

The Aptera also features regenerative braking, which is a technology used in most electric and hybrid cars. Regenerative braking both provides additional power to the battery and makes a vehicle more ecofriendly.

Aptera

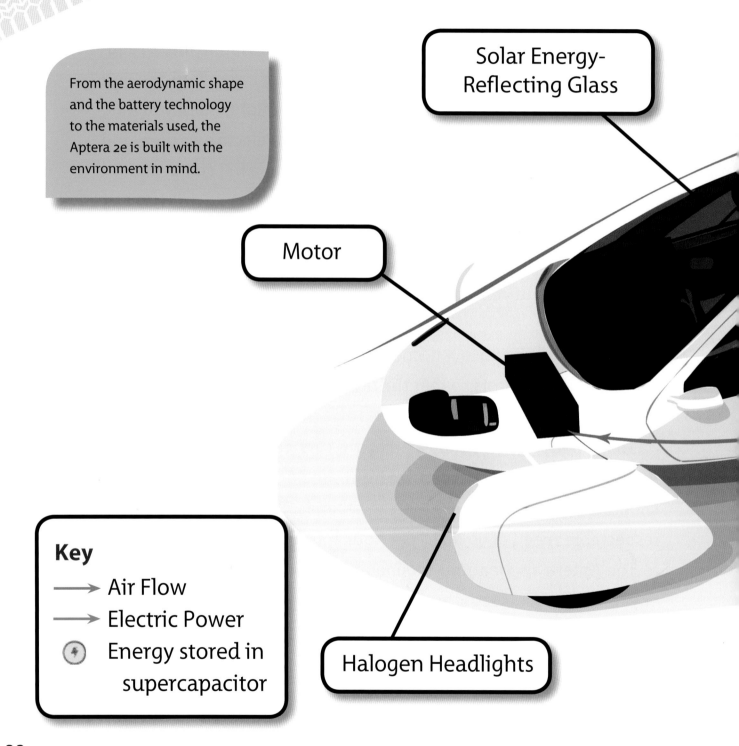

From the aerodynamic shape and the battery technology to the materials used, the Aptera 2e is built with the environment in mind.

Solar Energy-Reflecting Glass

Motor

Halogen Headlights

Key

→ Air Flow

→ Electric Power

⊛ Energy stored in supercapacitor

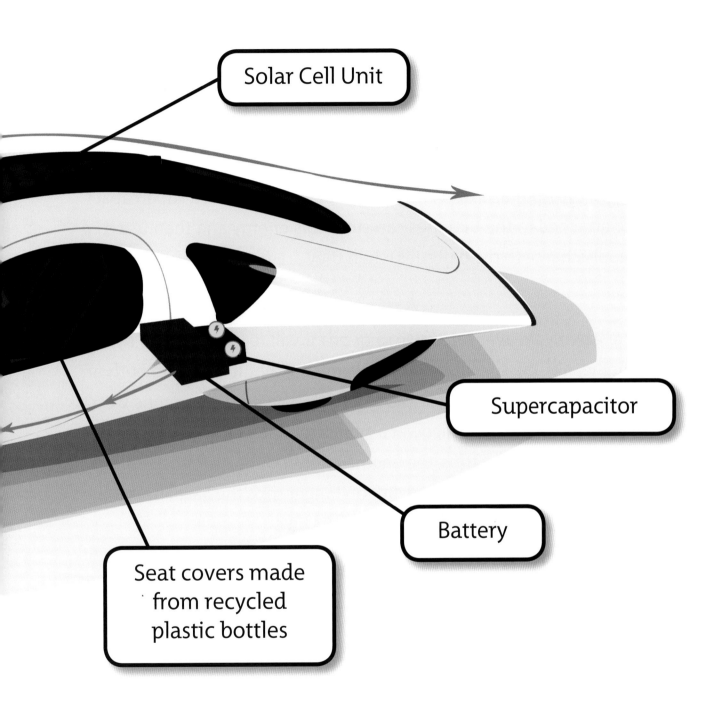

Solar Cell Unit

Supercapacitor

Battery

Seat covers made from recycled plastic bottles

When a car is moving it has **kinetic energy**. If a driver steps on the brakes, the kinetic energy doesn't disappear. It is actually converted into heat when the brake pad rubs against a disc that is connected to the wheels. This slows the wheels down and the car comes to a stop.

In a gas-powered car, the heat energy is lost to the air around the car. In the Aptera, however, an electrical device called a supercapacitor attached to the batteries can store this energy and then use it to supply charge to the batteries when they are running low.

Aptera 2h

The Aptera 2h, available in 2010 or 2011, will feature a series hybrid engine, like the Chevrolet Volt. This means that it will have both an electric motor and a gasoline engine. However, the gas engine won't power the wheels. It will power a generator that charges the batteries on the go. For short trips, the engine might not be needed at all. That means no gas would be used. But on longer trips the gasoline engine will kick in when the battery charge gets low.

The company says that the Aptera 2h will have a fuel efficiency of 300 miles per gallon (128 km/l) with a full charge. The car may achieve 130 miles per gallon (55 km/l) before it needs to be plugged in again. The run time on a single charge is much better than that of the Aptera 2e since the gasoline generator, which has a 5-gallon (19-liter) tank, will keep recharging the battery until the fuel runs out.

How Does a Battery Work?

Every battery—whether it's in a flashlight, a cell phone, or a car—stores chemical energy and converts it into electrical energy. This electrical energy makes the bulb in a flashlight light up, makes a cell phone work, and powers a car.

The Aptera uses a lithium iron phosphate battery, which is a type of lithium-ion battery. This means that the element lithium is the energy source for the battery.

A lithium-ion battery has two terminals called the anode and the cathode. When the Aptera is turned on, lithium ions (charged particles) travel from the anode to the cathode. This movement generates an electrical current, which streams through wires attached to the motor and provides power to the car.

Eventually, Aptera's lithium-ion battery will run out of juice and will have to be recharged. When a driver plugs the Aptera into an electrical socket, lithium ions move in the opposite direction—from the cathode to the anode. The battery stores this chemical energy and, next time the driver turns on the Aptera, will convert it into the electricity needed to power the car.

Aptera

The slender, curved teardrop-shaped body of the Aptera makes it glide along the road.

BEFORE THE 2 SERIES

The Aptera has undergone many different changes since the company first started working on the design in 2006.

The Mk-0 was Aptera Motors' first concept car, and it was able to get 230 miles per gallon (98 km/l) at 55 miles per hour (89 km/h). The car had a single-cylinder, 12-horsepower diesel engine with a 24-horsepower electric motor. The next model, the Mk-1, featured Aptera's new Typ-1 series design, but with a more finished look.

The Typ-1e and the Typ-1h were the first pilot models that the company planned to take orders for. The 1e was the all-electric version and the 1h was the hybrid model, which featured a gasoline-powered generator that would charge the battery pack on the go. The engine enabled the Typ-1h to achieve a much greater range: 600 to 700 miles (966 to 1,127 km). The Typ-1 series cars were designed with rear-wheel drive. The belt-driven rear wheel was powered by the electric motor and the front wheels were used to steer the car.

The Typ-1h had no side-view mirrors either, making it even more aerodynamic. Instead, the driver could see what was behind the car by using small video screens mounted in the dashboard. However, California state law requires the use of side-view mirrors, so these were added back into the design for the final production models.

Chapter 3

The Aptera 2e and 2h

Based on outward appearances, you would think that Aptera 2e and 2h are cramped, tiny cars. But once you slip inside the passenger compartment or look into the trunk, you realize that the company has done an amazing thing. They've created a luxury car inside an economy car.

The frame is made from a special honeycombed foam-core **composite** material (meaning the interior of the material is laced with a very strong structure of supporting cells). This structure makes the car's body six times stronger than steel, according to Aptera Motors.

The company is so confident in the strength of this material that it hosted a press event in March 2009 to showcase it. They invited

◄ **The solar panels on the roof of the Aptera power the car's climate-control system.**

The roof of the Aptera can support the weight of two full-grown elephants!

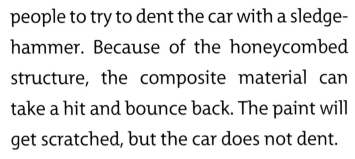

people to try to dent the car with a sledge-hammer. Because of the honeycombed structure, the composite material can take a hit and bounce back. The paint will get scratched, but the car does not dent.

The height off the ground is also an important safety feature of the Aptera. The car sits higher than most other cars' bumpers. If there is a collision, the other car's bumper will slide underneath the Aptera, **deflecting** the energy of the hit.

And if there is a direct hit to the front of the car, the Aptera's front impact zone, which is based on Formula 1 car designs, will help to deflect that impact. The side doors have side-impact beams to distribute the force of a crash away from the car's occupants, who are also protected by front and side airbags. As a matter of fact, the entire passenger safety cell is not only built out of the honeycombed composite material layered, it is also layered with strong aluminum.

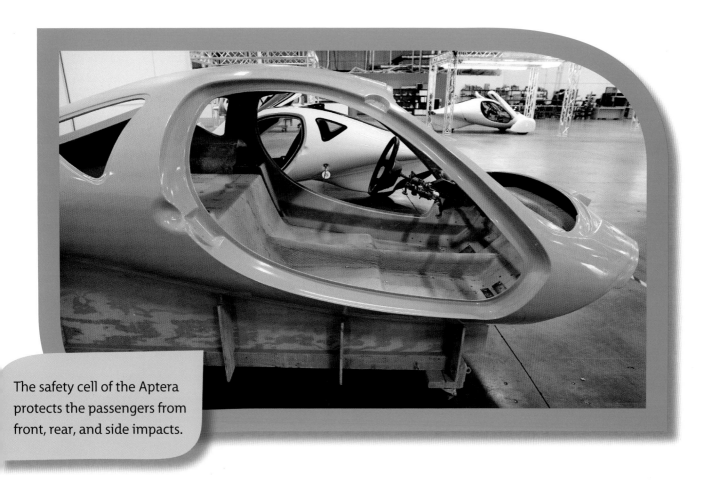

The safety cell of the Aptera protects the passengers from front, rear, and side impacts.

Atop the roof of the Aptera is a small solar cell unit. This powers the car's heat pump, helping to control the climate of the interior, even when the car is not running. On a hot, sunny day the fan kicks on and sucks hot air out of the car. On cool days the interior is warmed by the solar-powered heat pump. The windows are made from special solar-energy-reflecting glass, which also helps to control the car's interior climate.

Aptera

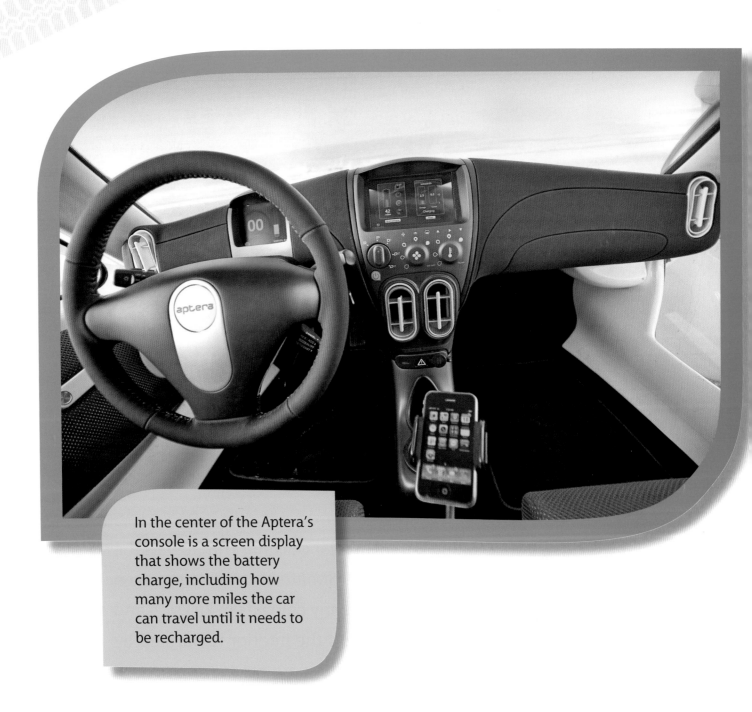

In the center of the Aptera's console is a screen display that shows the battery charge, including how many more miles the car can travel until it needs to be recharged.

The Aptera's dashboard is modest compared to that of other cars, but it offers enough gadgets and information to satisfy any car buff or technology geek. The Aptera offers smartphone connectivity and a GPS unit. There is also an efficiency meter that allows the driver to see how much energy is used as he or she drives. And, since the car is electric, a simple power button turns the car on and off.

The main controls are all together in a touch screen in the center of the dashboard. This includes vehicle systems information, the entertainment system, and a GPS unit.

The rearview mirror is equipped with a small video screen that is connected to a camera mounted on the back of the vehicle above the rear window. This gives the driver a 160-degree view of what's behind the car.

The car's two butterfly-style doors open up, not out like a regular car. Even in tight parking spaces the driver and passenger can open the doors without trouble. The doors also add to the cool, futuristic design of the Aptera.

Since the Aptera 2e is all-electric, it's a single-speed car. This means that the typical gears that enable a car to move forward, move backward, or park are replaced by three drive modes—D1 is best for long-distance driving, during which maximum efficiency is desired; D2 is for regular, in-and-out-of-traffic driving; and D3 is for faster driving, when quick bursts of speed are needed.

Chapter 4

Onward and Upward

Car lovers, and especially alternative-energy car lovers, are really excited to get behind the wheel of the Aptera. The company has started a reservation program, and they already have lots of orders. Clearly, the driving world is hungry for cars that are this efficient and cool-looking.

Aptera Motors plans to have both the 2e and the 2h available to consumers "sometime in 2010." The company estimates the cost will be between $25,000 and $40,000, depending on the options chosen.

◀ **The front view of the Aptera shows the unique design of its front wheels.**

Fun Facts

Does the shape of a car really make much difference in how efficient the car is? You bet! An average car traveling at 55 miles per hour (89 km/h) uses approximately 50 percent of its energy pushing air out of the way!

The company also has a gasoline-engine car in the works. While this car obviously will not get a fuel-efficiency rating as good as the 2e and the 2h, it will still be more fuel efficient than most other cars on the road.

Aptera Motors hopes to produce 5,000 cars in its first production year. They plan on adding a new facility soon that will enable them to build 20,000 cars per year.

Judging from the buzz the Aptera has created, they'll need it. Jay Leno, host of *The Tonight Show* and well-known car geek, has expressed his excitement about the Aptera, mentioning it on the program and calling it the coolest electric car ever.

Some other car companies—including Tesla, Chevrolet, Subaru, and Nissan—are working on all-electric cars, but few have advanced as far as Aptera Motors in having a car ready for production.

The interior of the Aptera is roomy despite its compact look.

Some, like the Chevrolet Volt (a series hybrid like the 2h), will be ready soon (2010–2011), while others are still a distant and expensive dream.

Aptera Motors is making founder Steve Fambro's dream of high fuel efficiency and independence from oil companies a reality—and wrapping it up in a cool package, to boot. The future is here. Or, as the captains of the *Enterprise* say when launching the ship into the frontiers of space: "Engage!"

The Aptera looks like a spacecraft on this California street.

Vital Stats

APTERA 2E

Battery type: lithium iron phosphate

Curb Weight: 1,500 lbs (680 kg)

Seats: 2

Top Speed: 90 mph

0–60 mph (0–97 km/h): 10 seconds

Battery Charge Range: 100 miles (161 km)

Recharge Time: 8 hours in 110-volt outlet

Glossary

accelerate   To move faster.

aerodynamic   Shaped so that air will easily flow around an object, such as a car, enabling it to go faster with less effort.

alternative fuels   Fuels that are less polluting than gasoline is.

atmosphere   The air surrounding Earth.

composite   A material in which two or more distinct substances—especially metals, ceramics, glasses, and polymers—combine to produce new structural or functional properties.

compressed   Squeezed together; in the case of the life-forms that became oil, they were compressed over millions of years by layers of rock and soil.

decomposed   Broken down into parts or basic elements; when plants or animals die, because of time, weather, and the action of insects and bacteria, they are broken down.

deflecting   Redirecting the force of an object.

drag   The forces that oppose the movement of a car. Also called *air resistance*.

efficient   Functioning without much waste or unnecessary effort.

environment	The planet's air, water, earth, and living things.
friction	The force, in the form of heat, that is generated when two solid objects rub against each other.
fuel cell	A device that changes a chemical fuel, such as hydrogen, into electrical energy, which can power a vehicle.
global climate change	A change in the overall weather patterns of Earth. Some changes occur naturally, while others are believed to be caused by pollution.
greenhouse gases	Gases, such as carbon dioxide, that contribute to global warming.
kinetic energy	Energy in motion.
organisms	Living things.

Further Information

BOOKS

Bearce, Stephanie. *Tell Your Parents All about Electric and Hybrid Cars.* Hockessin, DE: Mitchell Lane Publishers, 2009.

Famighetti, Robert. *How Do Hybrid Cars Work?* Science in the Real World. New York: Chelsea House, 2009.

Juettner, Bonnie. *Hybrid Cars.* Chicago, IL: Norwood House Press, 2009.

Welsbacher, Anne. *Earth-Friendly Design.* Saving Our Living Earth. New York: Lerner, 2008.

WEBSITES

Aptera Motors is the official website of the Aptera 2e and 2h. You can view images, learn about the technology, and post questions. www.aptera.com

Energy Kids, a website run by the Energy Information Administration, provides facts about energy use in the United States. http://tonto.eia.doe.gov/kids/

Energy Quest is the California Energy Commission's guide to alternative fuel vehicles. There is information on cars that run on gasoline, hydrogen, electricity, and biodiesel, as well as links to sources with more information. www.energyquest.ca.gov/transportation/

Science News for Kids's article "Ready, Unplug, Drive" has lots of information about plug-in and electric cars. www.sciencenewsforkids.org/articles/20081029/Feature1.asp

 Index

The page numbers in **boldface** are photographs, illustrations, or diagrams.

Index

About the Author

Tom Warhol has written several books, including *Eagles*, *Hawks*, and *Owls* in the AnimalWays series and the six-volume series Biomes of Earth for Marshall Cavendish Benchmark. He is also a naturalist and photographer with an interest in green technology and alternative energy.